A Woman's Guide to Improving the Relationship with Her Man

The Bumblebee Edition

KENNETH R. DICKERSON

Table of Contents

Introduction

This book is written as a self-help guide to help women understand the innerworkings, actions, and thoughts of men, in an effort to assist women at getting the fuck out of their own way. What do I mean by "getting the fuck out of your own way?" Women oftentimes ask, pray, and manifest for a "good man." But when that knight in shining armor enters her personal space, she retreats and says dumb shit like, "He's too good to be true." The purpose of this book is to help women understand what she can do to improve the relationship with whom she considers to be a "damn good catch." Of course, not all guys are created equal. Given a chance to live in a utopian world, many men will agree with the 43 opportunities in this guide to improve your relationship.

Everything in this book is based on my life and experiences with "Bumblebee." Bumblebee was a woman who captured my heart, mind, body, and soul from the very first message we exchanged on a dating app we met on. We had an amazing six-year relationship, but it ended in divorce. Getting a divorce is not the focus of the book. The focus of the book is divorce prevention; by highlighting some of the invaluable experiences I cherished with Bumblebee. My goal is to share my knowledge so you are aware of the things men desire in a relationship in the hope that you will not take those things for granted. Men should not take you and the qualities you bring to the table for granted either; therefore, you will notice I hold men very accountable throughout the read.

I have always subscribed to the number 3 being the perfect number. The ancient Greek philosopher, Pythagoras, stated the number 3 represents harmony, wisdom, and understanding. Additionally, the number 3 denotes the past, present, and future. This is the significance of the number 3 on the Bumblebee's back. Whether you're desiring companionship, casually dating, or already in an established relationship, I hope you keep the meaning of the number 3 in mind.

As you read this book, you will think that Bumblebee and I are still together because I chose to reflect on the good. I have a great deal of respect for her. She will ALWAYS hold a special place in my heart. I never thought I would meet a person with which I loved every strand of her DNA and be able to legitimately call her my wife and best friend. Thank you, Bumblebee!!!

When I refer to men throughout this book, I will use the term "we" or "us" because I am not excluded from the conversation. This book will make you laugh, cry, think, take ownership of mistakes you have made, and smile about the bullets you have dodged while fucking with some of our dawg-asses.

Warning…I use very colorful language because I want women to internalize what we're thinking, how we talk around our closest confidants when our significant other is not present. If folks are easily offended with the words and phrases of this nature, then this is not the book to read. I'm very educated, but fuck it…it's my fucking book!!! With that said, allow me to introduce myself. My name is Kenneth R. Dickerson. I am an author, educator, entrepreneur, and philanthropist. I am a veteran of the US Air Force and father to three amazing young women. I have an MBA and a Doctorate in Education. I'm extremely qualified about the topics in my book because I have lived it. I tell folks often, "Either I've run the game, or the game has been run on me." Another thing about me…I'm a Christian and mention God and religion at some points. Please insert any higher power you believe in, in those areas. By no means do I want to offend anyone, their faith, or lack of faith.

If you're still reading, then I hope you're ready to take this journey with an end goal of understanding the opportunities to find happiness with the man you desire. This is not a cookie-cutter approach, so don't get in your feelings and try to sue me if you don't find happiness; but rather check yourself and make some SMART (Specific, Measurable, Attainable, Realistic, and Timely) goals to attaining happiness with your person by completing the Self-reflection and Action Plan exercises after reading each "Opportunity." Remember, you can't please every man you meet; and every man you meet, won't please you. But I'll bet my good-ass government job check to a bucket of shit that if you seriously put the words you journal in the Self-reflection and Action Plan, you will be most prepared when HE finds you or to keep HIM (if you're already "booed up").

Remember That We Are The Dumbest Species On Earth

You read it right twice the first time. We are literally the dumbest species on Earth. I've seen nasty-ass Mississippi Delta mosquitos with more sense than we have sometimes. We're gonna fuck up, lie unnecessarily, get caught, then tell another lie to cover *that* lie up.

My friends and I hosted a pool party one amazing summer day. I asked Bumblebee to pick me up (8-minute drive) because I didn't want to lose my parking spot and needed to get the BBQ smell off me from cooking all day. This was to be a major moneymaker for us. She hemmed and hawed and eventually brought her fine ass to get me. At this time, none of my friends had ever met her. This wasn't because I didn't invite her to events and outings. It was because the most minuscule reason will cause her to cancel on me: "It's sprinkling outside," "The sun is too bright at 7pm in June," "You know my gout flares up when I'm around more than 50 folks."

When she picked me up, my friends were so excited to finally meet her. I pride myself on not ever taking off my ring, partly because I've cracked my knuckles so much that I couldn't get my ring over my knuckle, but mostly because I absolutely admired Bumblebee. So these cats come to the truck to meet her, and she puts on a brave face and a smile. Once I'm in the car and we're now enroute to our humble abode, she's goes off on me about people coming to the truck to meet her when she's not wearing a bra. I pop back with a phrase I've only heard white guys say on reality tv, "Why you acting like such a cunt?" What the fuck did I say that for??? She backhanded the earwax out of my ass. Why would I say something so dumb? I had no idea of Bumblebee's boundaries because I never asked — I assumed. As the old cliché goes, "Assuming makes an ASS out of U and ME." It validates my point that men are the dumbest species on Earth.

I humbly ask you provide us some grace when we say/do stupid shit. We sometimes have no idea of the ramifications our words/actions will have on you and the relationship. When we say something idiotic, ask us to think, then slowly repeat the exact same phrase again. In most instances, we will realize just how dumb we sounded.

SELF-REFLECTION AND ACTION PLAN

a. What was the dumbest thing a man has ever said to you?

b. What did you do in retaliation to that comment?

c. What do you wish you would have done instead?

d. What boundaries will you set in the future so men will not feel so comfortable making dumb comments (like I made) in the future?

MY ROAD TO HAPPINESS

To Hell With Your 90-Day Rule

First of all, this chapter is for those who are dating or at the beginning of a relationship. At one time, this "wait for 90 days to bump uglies" thing was a major spectacle. It was blown out of proportion by both men and women and literally unrealistic. Women had expectations to be wined and dined *only* for 90 straight days. Men assumed that by doing the wining and dining for 90 days, on the 91st day, the "cookies" should be automatically awarded.

Bumblebee and I immediately dismissed this concept. We both believed in not putting off sex to prove a point. We made a point to not pressure one another to have sex within a certain timeframe. When the feeling hit, and the mood was right, we were very confident that our sex would be amazing. In the event either of us was disappointed, then we knew how to tailor our conversations to discuss the ways to satisfy the other or walk away before feelings got too involved. We bumped uglies after the second date, and we were both very pleased. Our sexual values aligned, so our situationship became an amazing relationship.

I admire the sixth sense that women possess. Listen to that sixth sense. In most cases, I'm sure you can tell very early if you want to sleep with the man or place his ass in the friendship zone. It doesn't take 90 days to figure it out.

SELF-REFLECTION AND ACTION PLAN

a. What has been your experience with bumping uglies early in your situationship? Did you notice a difference?

b. How long did he hang around afterwards?

c. What has been your experience with holding out and not giving it up till later?

d. What factors will influence how quickly you consent to bumping uglies in the future?

MY ROAD TO HAPPINESS

Customize Your Relationship To Fit You, Not Society

I can't express how important this is. Bumblebee and I met on a dating app. I was very honest and upfront of the type of relationship I was interested in having...someone who's open-minded and fine with me participating in the swinger lifestyle, that I was accustomed to the majority of the 20 years prior to meeting Bumblebee. We decided on our very first date to have an open relationship. Now before you get to judging and shit, this is called having a true conversation and not sending your representative.

Of course, there were other suitors...some who accepted my lifestyle, some who didn't accept my lifestyle and figured they would change me, some who quickly moved on after the initial conversation, and then there was Bumblebee. She even went to a swinger club with me a couple times. Although we didn't participate with others, I was so grateful that she got out of her comfort zone enough to attend. She was the person I prayed for AND guess what? We further customized our relationship. I decided she will NEVER make a vehicle payment as long as we are together. I will be responsible for cleaning the home and ensuring that ANYTHING that's not operational in the home is fixed as soon as possible. There's a ton of other customizations we made that kept our relationship fresh and hard for the next guy to follow. I'm not sorry one bit for making the next guy's job increasingly difficult to keep Bumblebee happy in the future.

Let me warn you, it will be challenging to pivot from the traditional way of doing business in your relationship, but your relationship will be so much better once you let go of societal expectations. Others don't have to understand for it to make sense. Your relationship with your partner belongs to you and your partner. What others eat don't make y'all shit. I advise you to have conversations with your partner on how to establish boundaries when dealing with people who aren't supportive of your customized relationship.

SELF-REFLECTION AND ACTION PLAN

a. How have you customized your relationship to fit the desires of you and your partner in the past?

b. How did you deal with those loved ones who didn't agree with your customized relationship?

c. What would you like to do to customize your current or future relationship?

d. How will you deal with those loved ones who have an issue with your customized relationship in the future?

MY ROAD TO HAPPINESS

Don't Let Another Man Hate On Us

When one man has to put down another in hopes of getting an edge at anything (especially for some pussy), is a weak-ass man and will do some bitch-made shit sooner than later. Hell, a crackhead can't hide their crack habit for too long, so how do you expect a hating-ass man to hide his hating habit???

I recall being on the phone with Bumblebee while she was at the grocery store. A gentleman approached her with no clue I was speaking with her over her Bluetooth earpiece. This cat was really shooting his shot, even after she told him she was happily married. This man was being relentless, saying shit like: "Your husband can't take care of you like I can;" "He'll never have to know;" "I can pay your car note." Bumblebee finally asked me, "Baby, how much is my Range Rover note?"

As she switched from Bluetooth to speaker phone, I said, "You know damn well I paid cash for your truck but tell him he can buy the Bentley Bentayga you want." The next thing

I hear is, "That's fucked up to not tell me you were on the phone with your husband." "I guess it only matters 'cause you would not have been hating on my husband had you known. Sir, no one talks bad about my husband and how he takes care of me. You're dismissed," Bumblebee said.

I was so proud of her for sticking up for me. She knew loyalty is everything to me. That loyalty was one of the many qualities that drove me crazy about her. She held true to the words she spoke in her authored vows to me, "Forever I will protect and care for YOU, God's answer to my prayers." Bumblebee's actions matched her words, and I was grateful for that.

Loyalty is one of the greatest qualities we value in a woman…more than looks, sex, or smelling good. You should NEVER allow anyone to speak bad about your partner and vice versa. Not correcting a person who talks bad about your partner is likely to cause irreparable damage.

SELF-REFLECTION AND ACTION PLAN

a. Write about a conversation you engaged in with a hating-ass man while you and your guy were in a good place?

b. How did you handle the situation, and what was the outcome?

c. Write about a conversation you engaged in a with a hating-ass man while you and your guy were in a bad place?

d. How did you handle the situation? What was the difference in the conversations?

e. What would you do in the future if a hating-ass man approaches you?

MY ROAD TO HAPPINESS

_____

_____

_____

_____

_____

_____

_____

_____

_____

_____

_____

_____

_____

_____

_____

_____

_____

_____

_____

_____

_____

_____

_____

Love Me The Way I Want To Be Loved, Not The Way You Want To Love Me

Once we got to the LOVE stage of our relationship, Bumblebee and I had great conversations about what love looks like to us. We discussed our love languages and made those our barometer. My love language is Acts of Service. Bumblebee's love language is Words of Affirmation and Receiving Gifts. Below I provide only a few examples of how we decided to love each other.

Bumblebee agreed:

1. To take care of all my medical needs by booking appointments, educating me on what vitamins I need to take, and determining which medical insurance plan we should select to satisfy our family's needs. My dawg-ass didn't even understand the difference between a PPO or HMO before her.

2. She doesn't plan to cook every night, but she will make sure we always have a meal. I like to cook, and we shared those duties beautifully.

I agreed:

1. When I want to discuss something troubling, I was to give her a "sandwich" (say something nice, talk about the issue, finalize with words of affirmation).

2. Be sure to send her a menu when I'm out at a restaurant, bar, or any eating establishment. Bumblebee is the ultimate foodie but a homebody. I enjoyed making sure her pallet was always tested.

3. Provide regular gifts (no cost specified). I made it a priority to provide her gifts weekly. If she mentions that she likes something two times, she'll usually have it within a few days.

4. Maintain a vacation account for her by contributing at least $3k on January 1st of each year.

5. Rub her feet every night, scratch and oil her scalp the day before she goes to the beauty shop every week, and cut out her sew-in when it's time to have her new one installed (she considered this a gift).

We both were high on Quality Time. At a minimum, we decided: to eat dinner together every night when possible; cuddle after dinner; watch some of the shows she likes and some of the sports I like together; give 5 minutes of undivided attention to a conversation to check-in during our workday; attend worship service, pray daily, work out at the gym or at our home gym together, and go out on dates every other week.

Understanding your partner's love language is so important. Please do not take that for granted. To better ensure you're not taking this for granted, I recommend taking Gary Chapman's 5 Love Language Quiz and discussing the results with your partner. If he likes to be touched, "accidentally" brush against him when you walk pass. If he likes acts of service, offer to fix him a drink when he finishes his workday. You get it!

SELF-REFLECTION AND ACTION PLAN

a. What are some ways your man wanted to be loved and you made sure he was?

b. What are some ways your man wanted to be loved and you said, "Fuck that! I'm not doing that shit"?

c. Why were you not open to loving him that way?

d. Have you been open, honest, and deliberate with your intentions of how you want to be loved? If not, how will you do so in the future?

MY ROAD TO HAPPINESS

_____
_____
_____
_____
_____
_____
_____
_____
_____
_____
_____
_____
_____
_____
_____
_____
_____
_____
_____
_____
_____
_____
_____
_____

Stop Telling Your Friends All Your Business

Bumblebee's closest friends are so judgmental and opinionated about **everything** she does. They have criticized her taste in men. They have body shamed her. They have provided unsolicited advice about her desire to not have children. For those reasons, we decided to not inform her friends that we agreed to have an open marriage. I would hate for Bumblebee to ever be embarrassed if her friends were to know of our arrangement.

At one point in our marriage, I really had to self-reflect. I was dealing with several females who were in the lifestyle. I was moving like I was single. Although Bumblebee said she was fine, I wasn't. I needed to make a change. With her permission, I created a profile on a lifestyle-friendly dating site. Just my dumb luck, I matched with an associate of hers. Here comes these cackling-ass hens. Prior to this moment, they all were sweating me to hook them up with one of my frat brothers once they leave their husband (which I found incredibly odd). I prided myself on treating my wife well and being loyal to our custom-written vows. She was my person!

One of Bumblebee's friends called her at 6:30am and requested a meeting with Bumblebee that night. Although I didn't recall matching with her friend, I had a sneaky suspicion that I was discovered on the dating site. Long story short, this friend came over to tell us how our lifestyle was wrong in the eyes of the Lord....blah, blah, blah. My wife and I corrected the friend and informed the friend that this was the agreement we made from day 1, and that we were happy with our arrangement. Our relationship was customized to fit us. Our rules were simple, "We don't fuck with any ex AND no one should ever challenge our throne."

She even went as far as to say that she doesn't believe my wife will remain in this relationship. So, I had to act like Martin and told her to, "GET TO STEPPING!" (Clap two times if you remember the sitcom, *Martin*) I've never put a person who was like family out of our house. I must admit, it felt good...don't bring all that negative shit to our humble abode. Hold on, she was the same one who had a 7-year plan to divorce her second husband after her daughter graduated high school. I'll refer to her as "Eden" henceforth... with her dawg ass. I can tell that Bumblebee was emotionally torn. Does she remain faithful to our lifestyle, or does she FOLLOW her friend's guidance? I'm glad that Bumblebee chose me. The moral of the story is simple: STAY IN YOUR FUCKING LANE; THERE'S A LOT LESS TRAFFIC IN THAT MOTHERFUCKER!

SELF-REFLECTION AND ACTION PLAN

a. How have you reacted to friends giving you advice about your relationship regarding a matter you're aware of?

b. What are your future strategies to react to friends giving advice about your relationship regarding a matter you're aware of?

c. What do you believe should be off limits to share with your friends about your relationship?

d. Why do you think miserable friends interject themselves into others' relationships?

MY ROAD TO HAPPINESS

_____

_____

_____

_____

_____

_____

_____

_____

_____

_____

_____

_____

_____

_____

_____

_____

_____

_____

_____

_____

_____

_____

_____

_____

_____

_____

_____

_____

Be the Gina to his Martin

When you and your mate can laugh about ANYTHING and OFTEN, you better cherish it. I love to joke. And if I still didn't have child support, I would quit my job and try stand-up. I was divorced for 13 years before I married Bumblebee. I prayed for a specific type of woman. I was of the position, "Why keep asking the Lord for stuff when I was gonna do my own thing anyhow?" So I made a checklist… yep, a brother had a checklist. By the time I met Bumblebee, the paper was turned from white in color to yellow, 'cause it was so old. I digress.

I sought that love, chemistry, and connection that Martin and Gina possessed. *Martin* was a comedic sitcom that aired five strong years in the 90s. Martin Lawrence (Martin) was the leading actor. Tisha Campbell (Gina) was his co-star. Laced with satire and humor, Martin and Gina were in love. The way they loved each other and supported one another was priceless.

Bumblebee checked almost all my boxes. I wanted a partner that: was God-fearing, funny, intelligent, beautiful, family driven, with unchallenged pussy lips (you know there are some women with pussy lips that look like African ear-lobes), well-traveled, easy to talk with, compromising, open-minded, adventurous, who sucked dick on demand, had a great career, financially cognizant (not to be confused with financially responsible), understood sports, low on the drama meter, had realistic expectations about life, love my children as if they were her own, not intimidated by my level of education, patient with my adjustment from military life to civilian life...these are just some of the qualities on my checklist.

More than likely you will have to kiss a few frogs before your Martin finds you. If it hasn't happened already, be patient...he's out there. Once he shows he can be your Martin, please be the best version of Gina that you can be. It's extremely difficult for a good man to give his heart and be 100% vulnerable once he's been hurt. You're a wonderful woman and worthy of having a Martin you can depend on and be happy with.

SELF-REFLECTION AND ACTION PLAN

a. What qualities are you looking for in your "Martin?"

b. What qualities do you possess for him to consider you to his "Gina?"

c. What changes are you willing to make to be the best version of "Gina" you can be for your future or current mate?

MY ROAD TO HAPPINESS

_____

_____

_____

_____

_____

_____

_____

_____

_____

_____

_____

_____

_____

_____

_____

_____

_____

_____

_____

_____

_____

_____

_____

_____

_____

Foreplay Starts Before
We Get Home

When in a committed relationship, mental and emotional connections can often trump the physical. Bumblebee and I were having a conversation with my sister one day. She was telling us how she always gets dick pics. We asked her if she checked those cats. My sister's words, "Hell naw...I sent back a pussy pic. Ain't no point in having a dick pic without a pussy pic." On this topic, our prior home foreplay didn't include sexting, but it did include some graphic conversation.

But foreplay isn't always sexual. Talking about our day, what to eat for dinner, or our next vacation plans have all contributed to our version of mind fucking. These are things that turned us on. Remember to customize your relationship to fit you, not society. I conditioned myself to be turned on by what turns Bumblebee on. She often said that I "idle on horny," and that's because she did it for me. Just hearing her voice made my dick hard because I was that enamored with her. So for me, our foreplay started in the first few seconds of our call. The longer we conversed, the more I was ready to make her pussy leak either on my face and/or my dick.

Deciding what foreplay is appropriate is critical. The last thing you want to do is say some shit that you think is sexy but turns your partner off. Just as important, he needs to know what you feel is out of bounds, as well. I promise you; we will absolutely push the "boundaries" envelope. Give us an inch, and we will take 18 miles...trust!

SELF-REFLECTION AND ACTION PLAN

a. Have you and your man discussed how to turn each other on outside the bedroom? If so, what did that conversation look like? If not, how would you broach the conversation?

b. What are you willing to do and/or have done to show your man that foreplay started before you got home?

c. What are your limitations to sexting with your guy?

d. What would be your reaction if your guy sends you a dick pic that you didn't ask for?

e. If the chemistry is right and you're ready to take it to the next level, would you send your man a pussy pic/titty pic if he doesn't ask for them? Why or why not?

MY ROAD TO HAPPINESS

_____

_____

_____

_____

_____

_____

_____

_____

_____

_____

_____

_____

_____

_____

_____

_____

_____

_____

_____

_____

_____

_____

_____

_____

Use Fun Code Words And Phrases

It is extremely important to develop fun code words and phrases—even better—a unique language that is germane to you and your person. Below are some of the fun code words and phrases we established:

Fun code words/ Phrases	Translation
It's time to pay your bill.	Shawty, it's been a minute, and you need to break me off with some sex.
I don't have shit on shit.	We are minding our own fucking business and will not provide advice to other folks' issues; however, we will listen.
Do we have any bananas?	Grab your machete, 'cause I'm in danger.
What they eat don't make us shit.	That's their household, and we staying out of their business.

I'll get it back out you!	I guarantee you will give me what I want very soon, trust!
No angry dick tonight.	Whoever made you mad, don't take it out on my pussy.
Fuck those kids.	I love your kids, but I love you more. So if they ain't listening to your leadership and guidance, fuck 'em.
You've done more for less.	You let your ex cum on your face, but you say I'm your forever, and I can't?
We're too grown for peer pressure.	We're not about to let you or any-fucking-body else influence us to do some shit that's gonna get us in trouble in our relationship.
I don't need your help being a gentleman.	Get out of the way and let me open your door for you or lay my jacket down so you can walk over a puddle (in my LL Cool J voice).
Bless everyone on the highways and byways.	This is part of the prayer Bumblebee ALWAYS made sure to include before either of us went out of town.
If you don't tit, I won't tat.	If you start some shit, be prepared for my unlimited pettiness.

Using fun code words and phrases can make your relationship more stimulating and special. I recommend that when your partner comes up with a fun code word or phrase to describe something that you like, say to him, "That's a good one. Let's use that from now on." Little confidence-builders like that go a long way. Forever lasts a lot longer when you're getting along.

a. What fun code words/phrases have you established that will make your relationship fun for you and your partner?

b. What will be fun code words or phrases you would use so your partner knows that you're in trouble or not safe?

c. Would you recycle the fun code words/phrases that you used with your ex with your current or future partner? If so, why? If not, why?

MY ROAD TO HAPPINESS

_____

_____

_____

_____

_____

_____

_____

_____

_____

_____

_____

_____

_____

_____

_____

_____

_____

_____

_____

_____

_____

_____

_____

_____

_____

Be A Cheerleader

Cheerleading works both ways. I believe Bumblebee is the smartest person in the world. I've never met someone who has so much meaningless knowledge in their head. She's a walking Jeopardy contestant. That nerd shit is sexy as fuck. I 100% supported all her goals and dreams and shook the pom-poms without being probed. Whether she was writing an article, on a weight-loss journey, or wanting to give a few dollars to a family member; I had her back.

Most of the time, Bumblebee supported my dreams and goals. There was one time that she didn't. On Sundays, I take a couple hours to goal set and strategically think about what I can do to position our family in a winning situation. It was the spring of 2019 when I presented her with an idea to add to our portfolio of income. I wanted to enter into a license agreement with all the US major sports leagues and the National Collegiate Athletic Association (NCAA) to make face masks.

Think about it...how awesome would it be before you enter surgery, and your doctor is rocking a mask with your favorite team or college! Bumblebee is in the medical career field; therefore, her buy-in was extremely important to me. She didn't think the idea was a good one, so we didn't enter into that space. Fast forward to March 2020…COVID-19. Bumblebee felt so bad that she crushed a multi-million-dollar idea. From that moment on, she was definitely my cheerleader and trusted my business acumen. And that loyalty was appreciated!

By no means am I suggesting to go along with any and all of our stupid ass, get-rich-quick ideas. You not getting on board doesn't mean you're any less of a cheerleader. I advise you to conduct research and have discernment. Once you're comfortable and know that your man is not committing financial suicide, then wave those pom-poms as high as you can.

SELF-REFLECTION AND ACTION PLAN

a. What idea did your past partner have that you didn't support but later wished you had?

b. On a scale of 1 to 10 (10 being the highest), rate your level of cheerleading? Justify your self-rating.

c. How can you improve your cheerleading efforts?

d. What ideas do you have that you would like your current or future partner to support?

e. How have you communicated those ideas to your current partner? Or how do you plan to communicate those ideas to your future partner?

MY ROAD TO HAPPINESS

Compromise, Don't Settle

There is a very distinct difference between compromising and settling. To compromise, means to come to an agreement by mutual concession; therefore, both parties win. To settle, means to come to an agreement that either one or both parties will lose something. I believe Bumblebee and I learned how to compromise early. Of course, there have been times when we settled, but compromising is the preferred method. For instance, we compromised with our home. She paid the mortgage and house bills. I took care of all insurances, vehicles, home repairs, vacations, and groceries.

I understand that most men will pay the mortgage, but this method worked for us. Before you fucking pass judgment, I bought Bumblebee two Range Rovers in a matter of 18 months. I vowed to her that she will NEVER see a vehicle payment as long as we are together. If you're a homeowner, you can understand that shit breaks all the time. It was my job to ensure if something didn't work when Bumblebee left for work, that it was fixed by the time she made it back home. I took great pride in taking care of the house and Bumblebee.

I challenge you to fuck the traditional shit and compromise with your partner; otherwise, you're settling for the stupid-ass ideologies that may sink your relationship.

SELF-REFLECTION AND ACTION PLAN

a. Jot down the ways you have compromised with your partner in the past.

b. Jot down the way you will compromise with your partner in the future.

c. What compromises do you wish your partner had made for you in the past?

d. What compromises do you desire for your partner to make in the future? And how will you communicate this to your partner?

MY ROAD TO HAPPINESS

Don't Be A "Bug-A-Boo"

" You make me wanna throw my pager out the window. Tell MCI to cut the phone poles. Break my lease so I can move. 'Cause you a bug a boo, a bug a boo (bug a boo)" – Destiny's Child

To my young readers, pagers were these little electronic devices that beeped or vibrated when your friend or loved one wanted to send a message. Cell phones weren't really a thing during the pager days. So when someone paged you, left their number and added 911 to the end of the phone number, that meant CALL ME, IT'S AN EMERGENCY. MCI was a major telecommunications company that provided home phone service. Absent a phone pole, you would not be able to talk on your home phone. Back to our regularly scheduled program.

Revisiting Destiny's Child lyrics motivated me to write this chapter. No man wants a woman who is a fucking bug-a-boo. I must admit, Bumblebee possessed as little bug-a-boo behavior than any woman I've ever been in a relationship with. I believe that starts with trust. If you don't trust your man, then why are you investing any time with him? Like Lyfe Jennings sang in his amazing song *Goodbye*, "Once the trust is gone, you can never get it back."

When you call your man several times during the day, talking about, "I just want to hear your voice," we believe you're ear-hustling for background noises for another woman's voice. When you're at home and asking your man for a play-by-play of his day on a regular basis, we believe you're collecting information on our patterns, to use it against us later. When you're on social media interjecting yourself in all your man's posts, we believe you're trying to flex your dominance in the relationship. These are just a few bug-a-boo traits. We, men, can be bug-a-boos too. Look for the signs and steer clear of those types, or you may find yourself being the main character on the TV show, *Snapped*...and that person never speaks. I'm just saying!

SELF-REFLECTION AND ACTION PLAN

a. What bug-a-boo traits have you exhibited in the past?

b. How do you feel you have corrected, or should correct, those bug-a-boo traits?

c. What bug-a-boo traits have you past/current partner possessed that you know realize are red flags?

d. How have you corrected your partner's bug-a-boo traits? What was the outcome?

MY ROAD TO HAPPINESS

_____
_____
_____
_____
_____
_____
_____
_____
_____
_____
_____
_____
_____
_____
_____
_____
_____
_____
_____
_____
_____
_____
_____

Be The Perfect Balance Of Righteousness And Ratchetness

"Knuck if you buck." "I ain't never scared." "What you know about that?" When those ATL trap lyrics drop, Bumblebee loses her fucking mind. Her reaction to those songs would make you wonder how she is at the top of her game in the medical profession and can dissect the Bible as well as anyone I've ever known. We pump up the Sonos speakers to trap music at 7:11pm, then pray together at 10:03pm. This is what I mean by being the perfect balance of righteousness and ratchetness.

Be yourself but understand when to flip the switch. Your man wants a woman who is as diverse as his financial portfolio. Don't be ashamed to be yourself. Now, I'm not saying that it is ever okay to take a shit with the door open while your partner is at home, but let your partner know that you can hold your own in any setting and with any crowd. Feel free to watch the television programming that you like.

But also take the time to watch a football game with your man. This relationship thing is about give and take but most importantly PLAYING FOR KEEPS.

SELF-REFLECTION AND ACTION PLAN

a. What rachet tendencies do you have that you were ashamed of and hid from your past relationships? And how can you incorporate them into current or future relationships?

b. What ways will you incorporate your religious beliefs into your relationship in the future?

c. What rachet shit are showstoppers for you?

d. What rachet shit are acceptable?

MY ROAD TO HAPPINESS

Don't Let Anyone Else
Get You In Trouble

Literally, we are too fucking grown for peer pressure. Please don't succumb to other folks' misery, to the point that it influences your decisions and actions with your partner. This is one of the handful of times I will discuss a flaw of Bumblebee. She never understood that she's a leader in her peer group and often took the role of follower. More times than not, she fell into the struggle of groupthink and allowed others to dictate our relationship.

I recall a time when Bumblebee asked me if she could send her incarcerated cousin some money. I agreed to send $50 to his mother, who then would send him the money via whatever method she arranged with her son. As we laid on the couch after dinner (as we did almost every night), Bumblebee scrolled through her phone, and I noticed a Cash App receipt for $200. I asked her who she sent $200 to. She lied and said no one. She finally confessed that she sent $200 to her incarcerated cousin via Cash App to a number she was not familiar with. I was devasted. Bumblebee is not street smart. She has no idea if that Cash App to the unknown handle was to purchase Ramen noodles from the jail commissary, or to fund a contraband entering the facilities. This wasn't the first or last time I was lied to, and Bumblebee found herself in trouble with me.

The moral of the story is that you should honor your agreement with your partner. Loyalty is everything. There's no need to lie or allow other folks to infiltrate your union. Your partner is your number one, and when he's no longer your number one, let him go. He (and you) deserves to be a priority and not an option.

SELF-REFLECTION AND ACTION PLAN

a. Reflect on a time that you have allowed other grown-ass folks to peer pressure you to make a decision in your past relationship, and you regretted making that decision. How did it make you feel? How did it make your partner feel? Given your "friends" relationship status and past behavior, how do you now believe they felt when you chose them instead of your partner?

b. How will you handle grown-ass folks in the future who attempt to peer pressure you to make a decision in your relationship that you know you will regret?

MY ROAD TO HAPPINESS

_____

_____

_____

_____

_____

_____

_____

_____

_____

_____

_____

_____

_____

_____

_____

_____

_____

_____

_____

_____

_____

_____

_____

Don't Overprice Your Pussy

Living in a major city, I've often encountered women who have unrealistic relationship expectations. I've met women who were born-again virgins who had successfully delivered multiple children, never married, but expect the man to not have sex with her until marriage. I've met women who make $40k at the local grocery store but expect the man to make over $100k to support her and her children. I've met women who think calamari is a fancy word for chitterlings but would like to attend black-tie events with me. Or the classic women who expect the man to have a 6-pack, but she's built like a small Chevy.

In each of these cases, I feel those women overpriced their pussy and figured they brought more to the table than they really had.

There's nothing wrong with having aspirations and awe-some relationship goals; however, it's unrealistic to expect something of your partner that you're not willing to provide and/or do. Bumblebee understood this concept. She was down-to-earth and understood that it's not wise to believe her pussy was worth more than what she was willing to provide. She recognized I was just as much of a prize in her life as she was in mine. I loved the fact that she recognized my worth and wanted the best for both of us.

I believe some of the ratchet TV has negatively influenced the thought process (both men and women). It is very important that you understand where you are in life (finance, drama, baby daddy(ies), etc.) and how your partner will impact your being. You have to be real with yourself. Be who you are. If a joker gonna fuck with you, he will, no matter the baggage you bring to the table. His ass got some baggage too.

SELF-REFLECTION AND ACTION PLAN

a. Keeping it real with yourself, how have you overpriced your pussy in the past (i.e. had unrealistic relationship expectations)?

b. How will you adjust those unrealistic relationship expectations to be realistic relationship expectations in the future?

c. What unrealistic relationship expectations have past partners expected of you? What made those expectations unrealistic?

MY ROAD TO HAPPINESS

Be a Jump For, not a Jump Off

A Jump Off is a woman who is strictly used for sex, nothing more. We are not trying to make a Jump Off a priority. Let me be very clear, we don't consider you to be a Jump Off because you fucked before that 90-day rule bullshit. As I stated earlier, Bumblebee and I bumped uglies after the second date. I never considered her to be a Jump Off. Fucking early helps to determine if the sexual chemistry is worth the risk of exposing your heart to a person.

Just as most women realize early upon meeting if she's gonna give up the pussy; so does a man realize if a woman is a Jump Off or Jump For. We call the Jump Offs when our top 3 are too busy, super late at night, or after the NFL season has ended. Be real with yourself, either you've been a Jump Off or you had a Jump Off (commonly called a "Sneaky Link" now).

But let's talk about the qualities of a Jump For (in no particular order):

- One who doesn't nag but holds us accountable
- One who supports our choice of religion

- One who forgives
- One who is okay with being held accountable
- One who doesn't mute her smile
- One who respects
- One who will pick up the dinner bill every once-in-a-while
- One who understands the power of compromise
- One who loves unconditionally

The aforementioned is not an exhaustive list of qualities of a Jump For but shows the difference between what a man expects if he's to Jump For you. Bumblebee was an absolute Jump For...that person I lay down my jacket for so she can walk over a puddle. It is important to carry yourself as a Jump For. It's extremely difficult to put the genie back in the bottle once you cross over into the Jump Off lane.

SELF-REFLECTION AND ACTION PLAN

a. Describe the situation when you realized you were a Jump Off either emotionally, mentally, physically, or sexually? What made you realize you were a Jump Off?

b. Describe the situation when you treated someone as a Jump Off when they clearly believed the relationship was more than what it was. How do believe that person felt? How would you have felt if the shoe was on the other foot?

c. What will you look for in a future or current partner to feel comfortable that he thinks you're a Jump For opposed to a Jump Off?

MY ROAD TO HAPPINESS

_____

_____

_____

_____

_____

_____

_____

_____

_____

_____

_____

_____

_____

_____

_____

_____

_____

_____

_____

_____

_____

_____

_____

_____

_____

No Grown Ass Man Wants To Be Called "Friend"

That "friend zone" shit is for the birds. When a man feels that you, ladies, have turned the corner and now have "girlfriend-boyfriend" titles and you introduce him as a "friend," it will be tough walking that shit back. Bumblebee made that mistake once and only once. I didn't embarrass her and correct her in the presence of her constituents. We talked about it when we arrived back to her place. You see, that's the beauty of meeting a person you can talk about anything with. She didn't take my constructive criticism as a slight; she took it as my heart telling her that I don't want to be referred to as a "friend."

Keep in mind, she was my absolute best friend. But in the public eye, I don't want the moniker of "friend" attached to what we were building. Let me tell you how men think… if you consider us a friend to those closest to you, that says, "It's okay to keep fucking other chicks." We believe we are too damn good to be called a friend when we are holding it down. Don't be ashamed to call your partner "your man," "your guy," "your person…" anything but "friend," if you have reached that next level. Watch how his behavior changes when you claim his dawg ass.

SELF-REFLECTION AND ACTION PLAN

a. How would you feel if your partner introduced you as a friend after y'all had bumped uglies?

b. What does it take for your partner to escape the "friend-ship zone" and enter the "your man" zone?

c. How will you explain to your future partner that the road ends at "friends," whether you have bumped uglies or not?

d. How do you think you will handle the rejection if your partner tells you that he only wants to be "friends?"

MY ROAD TO HAPPINESS

Don't Mute Your Smile

Oh shit…I'm about to hit home with this topic. Many times, women want to mute their smile to their friends for several reasons. One being judgment. Fuck them hating-ass chicks you call friends. Real friends want to see you smile and happy. I recall when Bumblebee told her friends about me. Skepticism was their calling card. Ok…Bumblebee had kissed quite a few frogs in her time. When you look into a person's eyes, you can tell if they are genuinely happy or wearing a mask. I do not believe she was wearing a mask. Because those in her circle were both miserable and unhappy in their relationships/situations, it was unimaginable that their friend (Bumblebee) finally found a true happiness.

At the time we met, Bumblebee had never been engaged to, pregnant, married, or in a committed relationship. That's not because guys weren't after her, but rather she committed to her education goals and career. And before she knew it, life got away. So instead of celebrating her happiness, she was met with stupid-ass concerns because her friends were involved in dead-end relationships. This caused her to mute her smile.

Your man doesn't want his person to mute her smile for anyone. When you smile, I promise you, his heart warms. Your smile gives your partner reassurance that he's placing his eggs in the right basket. Your smile makes him want to share new experiences and build unique traditions with you. Your smile makes him want to do like Anthony Hamilton sings about in *I Know What Love's All About*, "Sending my life in a new direction, now I'm friends with my old man again. Standing here wearing this wedding band I can say I knew love because of you. Say I know love. I know what love is all about."

Smile…smile big and often. Fuck those who don't want to celebrate your joy. They probably just want your spot or want you any-fucking-way.

SELF-REFLECTION AND ACTION PLAN

a. Describe the time(s) you felt as if you had to mute your smile to your friends?

b. How would it make you feel if your partner muted his smile about you to his closet influencers?

c. Sometimes we have to learn how to smile again. What are some things that have made you smile with your past partners? Now, practice that with current or future partner so you can develop a habit of not muting your smile.

MY ROAD TO HAPPINESS

SPFEMS – Spiritual, Physical, Financial, Emotional, Mental, Sexual

As football coaches tell their players, "You better buckle your chin strap up for this one." Although we (men) are the dumbest species on Earth, most of us look for six attributes in a woman: spiritual, physical, financial, emotional, mental, and sexual. Your partner's value system will dictate the order of these operations. I will admit, Bumblebee and I never discussed our order. I wish we had, but knowing her, I'm confident my order is synonymous with hers. Allow me to explain how we (men) view each of these topics in our mate.

Spiritual – We want a woman who respects our choice of religious beliefs. This doesn't mean you have to believe what we believe, but simply show respect for whatever religion we have chosen to follow.

Physical – The first thing that attracts us to women are the aesthetics. Skinny, toned, or fat, if we are pleased with what we see; we will shoot our shot.

Financial – If a man has to come out of his pocket for every date, rest assured, he will not be around for long. We, too, want to feel like a prize and worth a few of the dollars.

Emotional – Yes, men are emotional creatures also. We want to know that you will love and nurture us. In return, we will protect you and our family at all costs.

Mental – Mental health is so serious. You'll have better luck convincing us to get a prostate exam before some of us will sit on someone's couch to dig into our brain. Men often feel that counseling is a waste of time and money. Until we go through something real, we don't understand the great benefits of counseling. Bumblebee and I were advocates of counseling (until COVID hit). We had some real breakthroughs and committed to quarterly counseling check-ins. This is another way we customized our relationship to fit us. Please don't neglect helping your partner to address past trauma. Until he's fixed, he'll forever be broken; leaving you to pick up the pieces through the totality of your relationship.

Sexual – Sexual chemistry is an absolute must in a relationship. I mean it how Gerald Levert sang it in *U Got That Love,* "I'm calling in sick to work kinda love." A man wants to ensure the sexual compatibility is on par before he commits.

I encourage you to delve deep into often having SPFEMS dialogue with your partner. We want to know that you care. Understanding your partner on a deeper level will provide you with the necessary ammunition needed when the road gets rough during your relationship.

SELF-REFLECTION AND ACTION PLAN

a. Of the six attributes described, which is the most important to you and why?

b. Of the six attributes described, which is the least important to you and why?

c. What other attributes would you contribute to this list to customize your relationship and why?

d. If you're currently in a relationship, which of the six attributes do you feel you need to work on with your partner?

MY ROAD TO HAPPINESS

Be Nurturing But Not A Slave

There's a fundamental difference between being nurturing to your man, as opposed to being a slave for your man. A nurturing woman does shit for her man because she knows that it will make him happy; so those deeds, therefore, make her happy. An enslaved woman does shit for her man out of obligation; receiving absolutely no satisfaction or a thank you from her man.

Bumblebee was extremely nurturing to me. I worked from home. Although she worked outside the home, she prepared my lunch pail, as if I was going to work at a construction site. She ensured I had vitamins, breakfast, snacks, lunch, and Gatorade. Absent a made lunch pail, I would either not eat or eat very unhealthily. She took great joy in making sure I ate healthy. I am forever grateful that she was nurturing and didn't feel that the services she provided were unappreciated or slave-like.

SELF-REFLECTION AND ACTION PLAN

a. How have you been nurturing to your partner in the past? How did it make you feel?

b. Write about a time when you felt as if the services you were providing was slave-like?

c. What nurturing acts would you provide in the future to your partner?

d. Based on your past experiences, what acts of service will you consider to be slave-like in the future?

MY ROAD TO HAPPINESS

_____

_____

_____

_____

_____

_____

_____

_____

_____

_____

_____

_____

_____

_____

_____

_____

_____

_____

_____

_____

_____

_____

_____

_____

_____

You Don't Have To Swing
At Every Pitch

Two positions in baseball are the pitcher and batter. The pitcher's goal is to throw the ball at a speed and velocity in which the batter will either swing and miss or not swing, and the pitch would then be called a strike or a ball. You see, the batter has the option to swing or not. No man wants a woman who swings at every pitch. This means you need not feel like you should provide a counter to everything he says. I'm not suggesting to be a verbal punching bag or feel you have to silence your opinions every time your man says something. I'm just saying that you should pick your battles wisely, so you win the war.

In the beginning, this was an area of concern for Bumblebee and me. She was very, very independent. That total independence comes with saying what you want, when you want, no matter if it hurt my feelings, or made me smile. Part of loving me the way I want to be loved (Opportunity 5), also means communicating in a way that makes both of us comfortable enough to express ourselves. This is how you fight fair. She eventually stopped swinging at every pitch; in turn, I learned to stand in the batter's box and take strikes and not say everything that came to my mind. This strategy helped me to gain a better understanding of the pitches she were throwing, which allowed us to have healthy conversations.

We prefer to not argue. The best defense is to sometimes drink a big cup of "shut the fuck up." Most women are so much better than we are at strategically picking the right battle enroute to winning the war. But those women who haven't mastered that art yet, are called SINGLE. If you feel something is an injustice, absolutely speak out and don't stand for that bullshit. When you find yourself having to swing at balls outside the strike zone, more often than not, it's time to find a new pitcher.

SELF-REFLECTION AND ACTION PLAN

a. Name three pitches you have swung at with a past partner that you regretted. What did you learn?

b. What three pitches have your mate swung at which offended you in the past? What did you learn?

c. What types of pitches can your partner throw in the future which you will accept?

d. What types of pitches can your partner throw in the future that you will NOT accept?

MY ROAD TO HAPPINESS

_____

_____

_____

_____

_____

_____

_____

_____

_____

_____

_____

_____

_____

_____

_____

_____

_____

_____

_____

_____

_____

_____

_____

_____

_____

_____

Offer Pussy Coupons

Ibelieved in doing things from the heart for Bumblebee, with no expectations of reciprocity. But very often, she let me know my actions really put such a smile on her face, and I was awarded pussy coupons. Pussy coupons are not some type of QRC code that can be redeemed by scanning. It's more like code that I know Bumblebee was gonna suck this dick like Ms. Pac-Man with a power pellet.

Pussy coupons, or whatever you want to call them, are such a turn-on to men. We want to know that we are desired by our partner. We want to know that whatever kind gesture we made really matters to women and not some check the box Valentine's Day shit. On second thought, I guess it would matter on the side-piece holidays…the day after the Valentine's Day and recognized traditional family holidays.

Back to the subject, awarding pussy coupons makes us feel loved, appreciated, sexy (even if we have a dad bod). Knowing our person finds us attractive is so important. We hear and receive that sentiment through pussy coupons. Of course, there are other things that turn us on and make us feel appreciated. But it hits different when a woman tells us, "Come home and redeem these pussy coupons!" You, too, might get a brand-new Range Rover…it worked for Bumblebee!

SELF-REFLECTION AND ACTION PLAN

a. What things can your future or current partner do to earn pussy coupons?

b. What sexy things would you say to your partner, so he knows he has earned pussy coupons?

c. What can your partner do to have you revoke pussy coupons? Meaning, what are some examples of things your partner can do to make you say, "I was wet and now I'm dry, because your dawg ass did that stupid shit."

MY ROAD TO HAPPINESS

_____

_____

_____

_____

_____

_____

_____

_____

_____

_____

_____

_____

_____

_____

_____

_____

_____

_____

_____

_____

_____

_____

_____

Be Real With Yourself

Fake hair, fake eyelashes, fake butts…reminds me of the scene from *I'm Gonna Git You Sucka*, when Jack revealed to Cherry that he doesn't have a 12-inch dick as he enticed her to bump uglies, and Cherry confesses that everything was fake on her body to include her left leg. I hated that Bumblebee felt she needed to wear fake eyelashes to enhance her amazing beauty. I hated it because every time she wore those fucking things, an eye infection resulted, so I was stuck using my Doctorate in Education to practice fake-ass remedies to heal her eyes. I don't a damn thing about medicine.

Women, dare to be different. We don't want women who constantly feel as if they have to "put on for the city." It's okay to rock your natural hair, whether you have edges or not. It's okay to say "fuck it" to those Snuffleupagus eyelashes…take them shits off. And keep your ass out the D.R., getting fix-a-flat injected into your ass. I promise you we rather you be real and not fake. That fake shit speaks to your character. In the words of the great Katt Williams, "Stretch marks mean one of two things. Either you was big and got small or you was small and got big. Either way we still fucking."

SELF-REFLECTION AND ACTION PLAN

a. What have you done to impress folks when you went out on the town? Why?

b. Why do you feel you must go out of your way to "put on for the city?"

c. What fake stuff will you stop doing, so that you can be your real self?

d. Explain a time when you had to take accountability for not being real with yourself?

e. How do you address you partner when he's not being real with himself?

MY ROAD TO HAPPINESS

_____

_____

_____

_____

_____

_____

_____

_____

_____

_____

_____

_____

_____

_____

_____

_____

_____

_____

_____

_____

_____

_____

_____

If Someone Isn't Feeding, Financing, And Fucking (3 Fs) You, Their Opinions Don't Count

I wish I could take credit for coming up with the "3 Fs" acronym, but I can't. All credit is to my frat brother, Jack, who I met overseas. Jack mentored and provided me with so much guidance that helped to shape my relationship ideologies. This is how this nugget was explained by Jack, "If a MF ain't doing the 3 Fs for you, then their opinions don't count." Basically, put "If a MF ain't Feeding, Financing, and Fucking you (and not necessarily in that order), then their opinions don't count."

Bumblebee and I believed in the 3 F's. It worked for us. We often said that we are too old for peer pressure. At one time, we consistently reminded ourselves that some people are in our lives for a reason and others for a season. I submit to you, reader, keep folks out of your house and business. Women share so much of their business with others who they believe have their best interest at heart. Those confidants usually do not, but rather want your place/lifestyle. A good way to tell if the previous statement is true is when your friend says, "Girl, if that was me, I would…" The moral of the story is, unless a person is consistently putting food on your table, paying your bills, and making you suck your thumb after bumping uglies, their opinion should not hold more weight than that of your man.

SELF-REFLECTION AND ACTION PLAN

a. How do you deal with those in your circle who have negative attitudes and are not doing the 3 Fs for you?

b. If you had to rank order your 3 Fs, which would be the most important and why?

c. Explain why you ranked the #2 and #3 "F" as you did.

MY ROAD TO HAPPINESS

Don't Expect A Man To Do Something For You That You Won't Even Do For Yourself

Bumblebee has never violated this opportunity. Countless times, she had sincerely reached for the dinner bill. Sometimes, she insisted to pay; but most of the time, I took the bill. It really warmed my heart to know that she wouldn't expect me to provide a financial obligation that she wouldn't take care of herself.

This opportunity spans past finances. It's also about loyalty, honesty, and respect. Don't expect a man to be loyal to you if you're out in these streets "kee-kee-kee-ing" in every guy's face that tells you that you're beautiful. Don't expect a man to be honest with you, when you're telling your friends one thing about him, but telling him something very different. Definitely, don't expect a man to respect you when you're living a fake-ass Atlanta's Housewives' life. You have to absolutely have to have your man's back if you expect him to show up for you.

SELF-REFLECTION AND ACTION PLAN

a. In the past, what have you expected a man to do for you that you weren't willing to do for yourself?

b. What has a man expected of you but wouldn't do for himself?

c. In addition to loyalty, honesty, and respect; what other attributes should your partner possess to make you want to go the extra mile for him?

_____

_____

_____

_____

_____

_____

_____

_____

_____

_____

_____

_____

_____

_____

_____

_____

_____

_____

_____

_____

_____

_____

_____

_____

_____

_____

_____

Don't Accept a Man Who Makes
Poor Pussy Decisions (PPDs)

What are Poor Pussy Decisions (PPDs)? PPD is a term Bumblebee and I came up with early in our marriage. It basically refers to when a man allows his smaller head (the one with one eye) to enter into some type of arrangement with a woman that 100% contradicts the decision his bigger head (the one with two eyes) would have made. PPDs are most often made when a man is under the influence of narcotics, alcohol, peer pressure, etc.

Given my lifestyle, I made a few PPDs early in our relationship. Nothing egregious, like getting burned, entertaining a stalker, or another woman calling Bumblebee. My PPDs consisted of dealing with women who weren't on my level – hood-ass women who I could easily influence to suck my dick in the back of the supermarket parking lot.

Basically, I moved at one time like my shit didn't stink. Because she allowed me freedoms to have extramarital activities with randoms, I did the most. I was wrong, arrogant, and took advantage of the situations. Once Bumblebee and I had a very real conversation about PPDs, the lightbulb went off. PPDs could have consisted of the egregious shit that I mentioned earlier, and maybe even more serious. It is my job to protect Bumblebee, and I can't do that if I'm making PPDs. I corrected my dumb-ass behavior. Every once in a while, before I left the home, Bumblebee's spider senses must have been twerking as she reminded me "No PPDs tonight. I love you. Have fun. Be safe." And those four statements resounded in both heads. I'll be damned if I will put myself in a situation to make a PPD. Don't accept a man who consistently makes PPDs. This rule applies to the casual dater as well. Practice doesn't make perfect; practice makes permanent.

SELF-REFLECTION AND ACTION PLAN

a. What egregious PPDs have your partner made in the past?

b. How did you react to those egregious PPDs?

c. What PPDs do you consider minor infractions?

d. What will you do in the future to prevent PPD infractions?

MY ROAD TO HAPPINESS

Keep Yourself In Shape

No man wants a woman that can't turn the head of another man/woman when she walks by...point blank, PERIOD. I often tell folks that if they don't get in the habit of working out early in life, as you get older, fitness and healthy eating will feel like a chore. Bumblebee struggled with maintaining fitness motivation.

Bumblebee has a number of grave health issues, which should have scared her into eating and taking care of herself better. At one time, I thought she was just being lazy. I had to take a step back and realize that she never has been and will probably not ever be a consistent gym rat. Ladies, you know how it is...once you get home and take off that bra, the rest of the day is history.

So, I decided to build a gym in the house. I created a workout plan that we can do together. We blocked off time in our schedules and committed to training together for at least 45 minutes 2-3 times per week. She started ordering meals from meal delivery services and started a recipe book. We ate from small saucers, instead of grown-folks' sized plates. Before we knew it, we were both getting in better shape.

When we stepped out on the town, she was looking so damn good. Shit, Bumblebee was stacked like dirty laundry in the projects. Trust, the guys were looking a lot, but not in a disrespectful manner. More so of a "how much did that ugly-ass dude pay her to go out with him tonight?" Working out with your partner will likely positively impact both of your self-esteems.

SELF-REFLECTION AND ACTION PLAN

a. What are some ways you and your future or current partner can motivate each other to maintain a healthier eating and fitness lifestyle?

b. How do you believe you will handle a situation in which your partner refuses to adhere to the agreed eating and fitness goals?

c. Understanding aesthetics are only part your partner's qualities, what physical characteristics would you like your future partner to possess, or current partner to work on?

d. Knowing that most of us are not the same size we were in high school, what body insecurities do you have? What are you doing to fix those insecurities (both mentally and physically), so you can become the best version of yourself for your future or current partner?

MY ROAD TO HAPPINESS

_____

_____

_____

_____

_____

_____

_____

_____

_____

_____

_____

_____

_____

_____

_____

_____

_____

_____

_____

_____

_____

_____

_____

Be Genuinely Accountable

A trait in a woman that I find tremendously sexy is accountability. I won't front, this was a sticking point in my relationship with Bumblebee. She had a real issue being called out on her shit. I'm not sure if it was because she sometimes felt her shit didn't stink, or because she truly didn't realize the power of apologizing for being wrong and taking true ownership of that mistake. To be genuinely accountable, means to accept total responsibility for your actions, as opposed to backpedaling, spinning, or being evasive.

I can recall a time when Bumblebee and I decided to allow her niece and newborn child to move into our home while the niece's newlywed husband was deployed. The niece was also employed. Together they made nearly $200k/ year. Mainly because they had a newborn, we wanted to do our part to help them save money, so when the husband returned, they could purchase their first home. Bumblebee and I decided to charge them a flat rate of $600/month. According to Bumblebee, all parties agreed with a hug. I did not participate in executing the deal, because Bumblebee insisted she does this alone.

Bumblebee and I were splitting the $600 in half, so she could put extra on the bills, and I could buy extra food for the home. On the third month of the verbal lease, Bumblebee only deposited $250 into my account. She told me that her niece was short that month. Literally, the next minute the niece walked in with a carryout of oxtails. WTF...something wasn't adding up. After a couple days of asking questions, Bumblebee finally told me the truth...she decided that the family will live with us for free, and she was transferring money from her account to mine, to cover up her niceness.

Instead of taking genuine accountability, Bumblebee was evasive for two days. Instead of taking genuine accountability, Bumblebee backpedaled and made every excuse in the book for lying. Instead of taking genuine accountability, Bumblebee tried to spin the story. This is one of the few negative Bumblebee stories I have in this edition.

Ladies, once you're caught in a lie, just take genuine accountability; otherwise, you will forever be lying to your partner. Those lies are not worth your relationship, if you truly respect your man. All things that happen in the dark will eventually come to light. Double standard alert...men struggle mightily with this same advice, so don't expect a miracle. I told you we were the dumbest species on Earth!

SELF-REFLECTION AND ACTION PLAN

a. What have been your past reactions when your partner refused to take genuine accountability?

b. How do you believe you will react in the future when your partner refuses to take genuine accountability?

c. Name three occasions when you didn't take genuine accountability with your past partner(s)? Why did you choose to not take genuine accountability? Collectively, what did you learn from the past that will help you in the future?

MY ROAD TO HAPPINESS

_____

_____

_____

_____

_____

_____

_____

_____

_____

_____

_____

_____

_____

_____

_____

_____

_____

_____

_____

_____

_____

_____

_____

We Like Mushy Shit Too

I'm not big on receiving gifts. I have an issue receiving things from anyone, mainly because I can't fucking stand folks throwing their kindness back in my face to guilt me into a future favor ("Remember when I gave you a pack of Now and Later when you was a kid? Now, let me 'borrow' $500). I truly believe any gift Bumblebee ever gave me was from the heart.

More importantly, she respected the fact that I'd prefer something mushy (i.e. card, love letter, text saying she loves me). Believe it or not, most men like that mushy shit. You doing that makes us feel appreciated, loved, honored, and revered. It makes us walk around with our chests poked out saying, "My chick is better than yours." You've heard it a thousand times, but it's literally the little things that count.

SELF-REFLECTION AND ACTION PLAN

a. What mushy shit have you provided to past partner(s) that were received well?

b. What mushy shit have you provided to past partner(s) that were not received well?

c. What mushy shit would you prefer your future or current partner provide you with?

d. What mushy shit would you prefer your future or current partner not provide you with?

MY ROAD TO HAPPINESS

_____

_____

_____

_____

_____

_____

_____

_____

_____

_____

_____

_____

_____

_____

_____

_____

_____

_____

_____

_____

_____

_____

_____

_____

_____

_____

_____

When Emotions Are High, Logic Is Low; When Logic Is High, Emotions Are Low

Naturally, women are emotional beings, and men are logical. This is not the case all the time. Depending on the situation, women and men have switched places. I recall a time when my emotions were high and logic was low.

She made a $3,200 purchase on my credit card, for which she was an authorized user. Our agreement was to consult with one another for purchases over $150 prior to placing said purchase on the credit card. I blew my top and went off. She tried her best to be logical, by admitting to her mistake and promising to make payments on the credit card until the debt was cleared. Me, being emotional about my funky-ass 820 credit score dropping to an 815 (anything over 780 is just showing off any-fucking-way), prompted me to remove her as an authorized user from my credit card without considering the ramifications my actions could have on her credit score.

I couldn't get out of my own damn way and realize the logic. After removing Bumblebee as an authorized user, her credit score dropped from Excellent to Good, with all three credit bureaus. I felt terrible because she had worked so hard to finally achieve an Excellent score, and I ruined that achievement with two swipes right on my cell phone. I eventually added her back and forgave her unauthorized purchase, but the damage had been done. It took a minute for me to build her emotional bank back up. I could have handled that situation better.

The moral of the story is, when our (men) emotions are high, we need your brilliant assistance in helping us recognize that we are being more emotional than logical. Giving us those gentle reminders, will help us make better, strategic decisions in all aspects of life.

SELF-REFLECTION AND ACTION PLAN

a. In your past relationships, have you been more logical or more emotional? Support your answer with an example.

b. How will you help your future or current partner build up his emotional intelligence, so your relationship is given the best possibility to succeed?

c. What has your reaction been to your partner being logical, while you were very emotional?

d. Write a letter to your future or current partner helping him understand three things you do when you are emotional and what he can do to help talk you off the ledge, so a compromised solution can be reached during conflict.

MY ROAD TO HAPPINESS

_____

_____

_____

_____

_____

_____

_____

_____

_____

_____

_____

_____

_____

_____

_____

_____

_____

_____

_____

_____

_____

_____

_____

_____

_____

A Man Will Change
For The Right One

My way, cheap, womanizer, lost, are only but a few ways to describe the way I was prior to meeting Bumblebee. I had no desire to change and often bragged that I was ok out here in these streets. I had no desire to love again. Like several men, I've been hurt, so trusting any woman with my heart wasn't really in the cards.

Then, entered this Pretty Brown Thang (PBT) who accepted me for me. In entered a sensual soul, with whom I can laugh, even at a funeral. In entered the heart catcher, who danced with me in the parking lot on our first date to Bruno Mars' "That's What I Like," while giving zero fucks about who was watching. In entered the most beautiful eyes that made me feel I can be vulnerable and let my guard down. Bumblebee was the woman I prayed for, and I was absolutely willing to make the necessary changes in exchange for her unwavering loyalty and the opportunity to give her all the joy possible on this side of the dirt.

Ladies, a man will change for the right one. If he ain't willing, able, and/or ready to change; you can suck the vasectomy out of him, pay his car note, take his mama to the local flea market every Saturday, or even fake like you like his bad-ass kids – but you can't do enough to win him. Just be your genuine, sincere, authentic self. You will know that you are as relevant as air to him just by the way he does those three Ps that Steve Harvey wrote about: "Profess, Provide, and Protect." When a man can profess publicly that you are the most important person to him, when he ensures that he provides for you, when your partner will do anything in this world to protect you, it is very likely he will make whatever changes necessary to keep a smile on your face.

SELF-REFLECTION AND ACTION PLAN

a. What actions have you taken in the past to try to change a man who wasn't ready to change for you? What was the result of that relationship?

b. How will you know that your future or current partner has made the changes necessary to regard you as his future?

c. When your future or current partner looks at you, what do you believe you will see in his eyes that says he will always "Profess, Provide, and Protect" you without trepidation?

d. Describe the conversation you would have with your future or current partner explaining the non-negotiable qualities you desire in your mate. How will you know if he has those qualities and/or are willing to make the changes, so a relationship can be established/remain?

MY ROAD TO HAPPINESS

We've Done More For Less

Bumblebee and I made a habit of thanking one another for acts of kindness that we often did for one another. Instead of always saying, "You're welcome," we would say, "I've done more for less." This means that in our past relationships, we each have provided more acts of kindness for folks who were either unappreciative or not worthy.

Bumblebee made it very clear that she had high expectations for me but is not trying to have me jump through hoops that the fuck boys, who weren't half as good, weren't required to do. This made me want to step my game up even more. I'm not saying to put yourself out there and repeat failed episodic events. My position is that a damn good man knows he's as much of a prize as you believe he is.

Let that sink in…You've done MORE for LESS. You've probably sucked your past partner off regularly and couldn't even get $5 for a two-piece and biscuit at Church's. But you get a damn good man and expect him to take your kids to Chuck E. Cheese, and you won't even give him a hand job. Damn good men peep that shit so early. Don't mess around and lose a damn good man because you're holding him accountable for some bullshit "Tyrone" put you through. But definitely hold him accountable for the arrangements you have agreed to in your relationship.

SELF-REFLECTION AND ACTION PLAN

a. What type of great things have you done for your past partner, knowing damn well the relationship would not last? Why did you do those things?

b. What type of great things have you expected of a past relationship that you didn't require of relationships prior?

c. What realistic actions are you willing to do for a damn good man?

d. Write about a time you lost a damn good man because of your unrealistic expectations? If you could talk to your younger self, what would you tell yourself to do differently?

MY ROAD TO HAPPINESS

_____

_____

_____

_____

_____

_____

_____

_____

_____

_____

_____

_____

_____

_____

_____

_____

_____

_____

_____

_____

_____

_____

_____

_____

_____

Understand Pet Peeves

Just as it's important to know what makes us happy, it's equally as important to know what pisses us off. As explained earlier, Bumblebee had never been in a committed relationship prior to our marriage, when she was 43 years young (hence, 43 chapters in this book). Therefore, I had to be prepared for the strong possibility that she was set in her ways. And that she was.

In my opinion, you shouldn't ever commit to someone until you witness that person experiencing some type of adversity. The only way to do that is to understand your partner's pet peeve. Mine are very simple:

1. Don't ignore me.
2. Don't answer my question with a question. When you violate this, you're on the road to #3.
3. Don't be evasive. Being evasive places women on defense and leads to #4.
4. Don't lie to me or call me a liar, without proof.
5. This has nothing to do with 1-4; but not recognizing my worth or taking me for granted.

SELF-REFLECTION AND ACTION PLAN

a. What are your pet peeves?

b. What past experiences helped you to land on those pet peeves?

c. What communication strategies will you use to inform your future or current partner that he had violated your pet peeves?

d. How many violations of your pet peeves will encourage you to end the relationship?

e. What will you do to better understand your partner's pet peeves, so you don't violate them?

MY ROAD TO HAPPINESS

_____

_____

_____

_____

_____

_____

_____

_____

_____

_____

_____

_____

_____

_____

_____

_____

_____

_____

_____

_____

_____

_____

_____

_____

_____

Sexual Value Systems...Have That Talk Early And Often

Have you ever been with a person who valued something like hunting, and you absolutely despise the wild? This is just one of the many value systems your partner may possess, which is likely different than yours. Usually, when folks speak about value systems, they are referring to religion, family, finances, or those 3-4 words in a company's strategic plan that you memorize prior to interviewing for a job, so you can impress the panel that you know something about the company (known as core values). I'm taking another route...I want to talk about sex.

As with most couples, Bumblebee and I started out hot and heavy...bumping uglies 4-5 times per week. The humping like rabbits eventually dwindled. Although we talked about and agreed to the open relationship concept, I feel her sexual value system was not in 100% alignment with mine. I believed Bumblebee to be the sexiest woman on Earth, even prior to the cosmetic surgeries. After coming home from the swinger's club, I showered before coming to bed. Her sexy ass would be lying there, sleep in the nude, and before you know it, that dick was hard again, as if I didn't just bust three times before coming home. The point is, that I was extremely attracted to Bumblebee...clothes on or naked.

Her sexual value system's position was that I should be satisfied, because I'd been fucking a good portion of the evening. My sexual value system's position was like, "Sure, but right now I want to make love to my queen." Eventually, I decided to SHAC (SHut-up And Color) and waited on her to tell me, "It's time to pay your bill." I adjusted my sexual value system to be more aligned with hers. This was an absolute settlement, not a compromise. I believe had we been more honest about our sexual value systems, we would possibly still be a couple today. I challenge you to understand your partner's sexual value system and allow him to understand yours. This will help to avoid a lot of confusion and sexual misunderstanding in the future. I take full accountability for not addressing this with Bumblebee earlier.

SELF-REFLECTION AND ACTION PLAN

a. What does your sexual value system consist of (e.g. oral, anal, more than 8-inches, group, toys, 7 days a week, etc.)?

b. What ways would you alter your sexual value system for your future or current partner? This means what have you not done, or did very infrequently, that you're willing to do regularly - if your future or current partner desires it?

c. Write about a time when you knew that your sexual value system did not match with your past partner, but y'all chemistry was so fucking dope. Did you address and stay, ignore and stay, address and leave, or ignore and leave? What factors influenced that decision?

MY ROAD TO HAPPINESS

Simple Questions Require Simple Answers

Men desire simple answers to our simple questions. We are not as complex of communicators as y'all. We can barely process one question at a time in a relationship but find ourselves multitasking all the time at work...go figure. In our relationships, we prefer simple answers when we ask simple questions. Let's take the example below:

Me: I would like you to treat you to dinner tonight. What you want to eat?

Bumblebee: It doesn't matter.

Me: Okay, I'll get a salad from that place you like.

Bumblebee: Naw, I don't want that.

Me: What do you have a taste for?

Bumblebee: Anything but salad.

Me: How about fried chicken from that place near the gym?

Bumblebee: Not that either.

Me: Okay, PBT, just order something. I'll pick it up. I'm leaving the gym in about 20 minutes. Use my card because I'm treating you.

<5 minutes later>

Bumblebee: I just saw a commercial, and the Asian Zensation Zalad is back at Zaxby's. The order will be ready in 15 minutes.

Me: Did you get chicken on the salad?

Bumblebee: Of course, I got fried chicken…that's what makes the Zalad Zensation.

Women are known to have multiple conversations with us at the same time. We can keep up with the multiple conversations as much as a person with no legs can ice skate uphill. For instance, if we ask about your day; we just want the simple answer; not about your friends, the next movie coming out, or explaining a concept that only you and a Jeopardy player understand. We want to know about your day first, THEN go into all that other stuff. I promise you, that behavior will stop us from asking you how's your day.

SELF-REFLECTION AND ACTION PLAN

a. Reflect on the conversation Bumblebee and I had. How do you think your past partner would have felt after this exchange?

b. When you recognize that your future or current partner is seeking a simple answer, but you're already knee-deep in a complex answer; what will you do to make sure he receives the simple answer?

c. Name three adjectives that describe how you felt when your past partner started answering your simple question with complex answers? What past behaviors (either yours or his) impacted the reason for using those adjectives?

MY ROAD TO HAPPINESS

_____

_____

_____

_____

_____

_____

_____

_____

_____

_____

_____

_____

_____

_____

_____

_____

_____

_____

_____

_____

_____

_____

_____

Strive To Be As Evenly Yoked
As Possible

When a couple decides to split up, one of the first things the "street committee" starts to gossip is, "They didn't make it, because they were unevenly yoked." Although Bumblebee and I had a ton in common and would complete each other's sentences several times daily, we were very different. She's a die-hard 90s hip-hop head; I'm into blues. She's a foodie; I eat to sustain. She will go up and down every aisle at the grocery store; I strictly shop from a list. So, does that mean we weren't equally yoked?

Time for the educator to teach: According to Merriam-Webster, a yoke is a wooden bar or frame by which two draft animals (such as oxen) are joined at the heads or necks for working together. The yoke is used so the oxen could work as a team to plow the land, side-by-side. Often time, one ox would be stronger than the other, which meant the stronger ox would pull the weaker ox along. The solution here is for the stronger ox to decrease its strength, so the weaker ox can increase theirs.

This doesn't mean the stronger ox's muscles will deteriorate. It means that the stronger ox will be throttling back from 100% to 90%, so the weaker ox could catch up. The weaker ox may never be as strong as the stronger ox, but that will be their secret. This is my interpretation of being as evenly yoked as possible.

I'm an American football fanatic and have enjoyed the sport my entire life. Bumblebee knew her fair share about football but would probably never know as much as I know. I realized that and was able to explain the game to her in a way she could receive and appreciate my affinity for the sport. In turn, she did the exact same to help me understand the entertainment value of "ratchet tv." It is extremely important you help our dawg asses understand that it is okay to not be the strongest all the time. This is the only way the TEAM will win.

SELF-REFLECTION AND ACTION PLAN

a. What does "as evenly yoked as possible" mean to you?

b. In what ways have you decreased in the past in order for your partner to increase?

c. In what ways have your partner decreased in the past for you to increase?

d. Name five areas of weakness that you would like your future or current "strong ox" to assist you with, so the TEAM will win.

MY ROAD TO HAPPINESS

_____

_____

_____

_____

_____

_____

_____

_____

_____

_____

_____

_____

_____

_____

_____

_____

_____

_____

_____

_____

_____

_____

_____

If He Needs To Consistently Validate You, You Ain't Ready

There's a fundamental difference between affirmation and validation. Affirmation is saying something like, "I appreciate you." Validation is saying something like, "Of course, I'll never leave you for another woman." I've been with several women prior to Bumblebee, and it seems as if many of them needed more validation and less affirmation. Bumblebee got it…she just fucking got it. She didn't need validation that often. She desired words of affirmation, so she knows that I realize her effort, her desire to be a great helpmate, her dedication to our future.

When you need extra validation, it pushes us away and comes across as needy. Of course, we want you to be somewhat dependent on us. But being overly dependent will make us sit in the car in the driveway after work, dreading to come in the house to start the evening with you and the kids. Please do not masquerade those areas where you need validation, because they will eventually become very obvious. Your partner will appreciate your willingness to be vulnerable. The hope is that over time you will require less validation and more affirmation.

SELF-REFLECTION AND ACTION PLAN

a. Name three ways you would like your future or current partner to show that he appreciates you.

b. Name three times you have needed validation in your past relationship. What will you look for, or do differently, with your future or current partner?

c. In what ways will you make sure your future or current partner knows that you appreciate him?

d. What has been your reaction to past partners who needed consistent validation? How did it make you feel?

MY ROAD TO HAPPINESS

_____

_____

_____

_____

_____

_____

_____

_____

_____

_____

_____

_____

_____

_____

_____

_____

_____

_____

_____

_____

_____

_____

_____

Keep In Mind The Accounting Relationship Principles

One of the first classes I enrolled in in undergrad was Accounting 101. In that course, I learned the basic accounting principle: Assets = Liabilities + Stakeholder's Equity. This principle can be applied to any relationship. Whether it's with your begging-ass cousin, clout-chasing boss, or your person…the principles can be applied. Of all the women I've been with, Bumblebee was the absolute best to understand my accounting relationship principle. Like any other equation, the left side must equal the right side.

Allow me to break down an accounting financial principle. Bumblebee wants a pair of boots that cost $100. This is the left side of the equation, known as Assets. She only has $70. This is one variable on the right side of the equation, Liabilities. Because I'm intentionally invested in every part of this woman's existence, especially her happiness, I will add the $30 in the form of Stakeholder's Equity. Now, the left side of the equation equals the right side, and Bumblebee has the boots she desires and deserves.

On to the accounting relationship principle I've coined. To keep Bumblebee happy, her emotional bank needs to be 100 (Assets). Let's say she had a bad day; her emotional liability may be 40 (Liabilities). That means I need to contribute 60 in Stakeholder's Equity. You may ask how do I account for Stakeholder's Equity? It may be listening to her while I rub her feet and watching one of the pre-recorded pictures (my Mississippi country lingo snuck out) on the DVR. It may be cooking her favorite meal (liver, rice, gravy, and sauteed onions) while she has a glass of wine and chats with one of her closet friends. It may be making myself go missing for the first hour of her being home, so she can decompress and rub one out with one of those battery-operated friends that live in her nightstand. Whatever it is, we need your help to understand the amount of Stakeholder's Equity we need to contribute, so that we can help you maximize your Assets and minimize your Liabilities. We want to know how we can best support you in all ways, so we can be the best for you and the family.

SELF-REFLECTION AND ACTION PLAN

a. How would you like your future or current partner to contribute Stakeholder's Equity? Why did you make that choice?

b. Being completely honest with yourself, what Assets do you bring to a relationship that you feel makes you a good catch?

c. Keeping it 100, what Liabilities do you bring to the relationship that you expect your future or current partner to accept?

d. How would you apply my accounting relationship principle to your future or current relationship?

MY ROAD TO HAPPINESS

_____

_____

_____

_____

_____

_____

_____

_____

_____

_____

_____

_____

_____

_____

_____

_____

_____

_____

_____

_____

_____

_____

_____

_____

Bring Your Own Confidence To The Relationship

Even a crackhead can't hide an addiction for more than 90 days, so why do you think you can stand behind a veil of misconceptions to hide your confidence? I saw very early that Bumblebee had some issues that she had yet to deal with. She allowed her personality to mask the pain, shame, and hurt that she had carried over the years. Her ability to compartmentalize past behaviors is second to none. But that compartmentalization shook her confidence, not her self-esteem.

When you don't bring your own confidence to the relationship, we, men, are held holding the bag and liable for the shit the last relationships put you through. Understandably, you don't want to be a fool again or relive a terrible episode, but the new guy didn't do it to you. It is so wrong to hold him accountable for what past dawg ass guys did.

On several occasions, I recommended that Bumblebee enroll and actively participate in professional counseling. Bumblebee is a very prideful person who believed she had it all together, and her mirror remained rose-colored.

Eventually, she realized those rose-colored mirrors were filled with more film than a 1970 Kodak warehouse.

Bumblebee's self-awareness helped to create a relationship of honesty within herself. Being able to communicate about your confidence issues and self-awareness to your future partner is very important in keeping him happy. I can understand the trepidation. Some guys will use those nuggets of openness as an opportunity to capitalize, manipulate, and hold against you. Guess what...if you bring your own confidence to the relationship, your energy won't even allow you to be attracted to jokers like that. So if you're already in a relationship, you can feel safe to work on your confidence; and if you're looking for one, know that this is a very important piece of the puzzle to work on.

SELF-REFLECTION AND ACTION PLAN

a. What confidence issues do you have?

b. What are you doing to become more confident?

c. Make a list of the things you are now self-aware of but were too embarrassed of or not comfortable enough to share with your past partner(s).

MY ROAD TO HAPPINESS

_____

_____

_____

_____

_____

_____

_____

_____

_____

_____

_____

_____

_____

_____

_____

_____

_____

_____

_____

_____

_____

_____

_____

_____

_____

Make It Hard For Another
Woman To Ever Follow You

" Don't threaten me with a good time!" I've often said that
to Bumblebee. That woman had a way of making me feel
like I was the luckiest man in the world. For men, it's the little
things that count...making sure there's always shit paper in
the house, asking about our day, reminding us to fast before
going to the doctor the next day. Then there are the big things
that she would do that made it hard for any other woman to
follow...praying with me and for others, ensuring that my
sexual desires are met, communicating about our long-term
careers and personal goals, and establishing a legacy.

We appreciate a woman who is willing to make critical
sacrifices. Those sacrifices put us in a place of vulnerability.
Fun fact...we want to be vulnerable. We want to open up to
you and for you to be a sounding board. We want to vent.
We desire a partner who will allow us to sometimes have a
one-way conversation, which means no interruptions. Early
in our relationship, Bumblebee mastered that art. I'm forever grateful to her for showing me that the next woman

should, at a minimum, match the energy and patience she had. Ladies, please remember that you don't have to be a world beater, just be better than the last chick in our life.

SELF-REFLECTION AND ACTION PLAN

a. What things have you done to make sure that your part-
    ner understands that you're trying to make it hard on the
    next chick?

b. What small things will you do for your future or cur-
    rent partner, so he understands you're making it hard for
    another to follow you?

c. What critical sacrifices are you willing to make for your
    future or current partner, so he feels comfortable being
    vulnerable?

MY ROAD TO HAPPINESS

_____

_____

_____

_____

_____

_____

_____

_____

_____

_____

_____

_____

_____

_____

_____

_____

_____

_____

_____

_____

_____

_____

_____

_____

_____

_____

Stop Second-Guessing And Correcting Us All The Time

Understanding that men are the dumbest species on Earth, doesn't give you a green light to second-guess us or correct us whenever you believe we are in error. Early on, I had real concerns that Bumblebee and I wouldn't work. She's super intelligent, and I'm slightly above average. I'm the type of guy who is extremely self-aware. Unlike some guys who have a terrible sense of direction, I will literally ask a crackhead at a gas station for directions. I'm so bad, that I had to use GPS just to get to the bathroom at our house.

Back to the subject…it's disheartening and makes us feel as if we're walking on eggshells, if we feel we have to be perfect each and every time we speak to you. Allow us to get things wrong sometimes. That's how we learn. The statements, "Are you sure?" "I don't know if that's the right answer," "I don't know about all that," spoken by you, to us, will send our dawg asses into a tailspin, resulting in us looking for your replacement. Sometimes you have to drink some prune juice and let that shit go. We, men, are prideful beings.

I understand that we can't be wrong all the time, so learn to give your man a small attaboy for being right sometimes.

SELF-REFLECTION AND ACTION PLAN

a. In your past relationships, what were some of the topics you have been known to often second-guess and correct your partners?

b. How would you use tact to second-guess and/or correct your partner in the future?

c. How do you feel when your past partners have frequently second-guessed and/or corrected you?

d. What strategies will you use to acknowledge when your future or current partner is being right?

MY ROAD TO HAPPINESS

Actions Speak Louder Than Words...Hold Us Accountable

A real man will not send his representative, even if that representative increases his chance of getting in between your legs sooner than later. At one time or another, most of us have not been real men and introduced you to our representatives. Most likely, you have met a representative when we felt you were out of our league.

Although beautiful and extremely intelligent, I NEVER believed Bumblebee was out of my league. I felt we were as evenly matched as a couple could be. I made a promise to myself to not lie to her and keep it a buck as often as possible. The exception being when I'm attempting to provide a joyous surprise. Any other lie to Bumblebee is as wrong as a fat vegan. Therefore, Bumblebee was at peace with the fact that my words matched my actions.

Women always say, "Actions speak louder than words," but are reluctant to hold us accountable. If we tell you that we're gonna take out the trash after dinner, don't let our dawg ass get on the PS5 prior to doing so. If we say that we're gonna eat that pussy like you never had it eaten before, eat a non-gassy lunch and sprinkle some of that good smelling Bath and Body Works "dust" down below to prepare for your oral sessions, and make sure we follow through. If we say that we say we're gonna take you on a vacation in 9 months, make us start a new bank account in which we are to make monthly contributions to ensure the vacation happens. If he says that he's gonna get a divorce, book him an appointment with an attorney (more than a few of y'all can relate to that one). Words with no actions are as useful as a butter-bean sandwich, and sometimes we need to be told to follow our words with actions. You must decide when you're tired of giving our dawg ass a pass for the misalignment of words to actions.

SELF-REFLECTION AND ACTION PLAN

a. Name three things your past partner told you and his actions didn't match. Why were you so accepting?

b. Name three things you told your past partner, but your actions didn't match. Why did you choose to not align your words with your actions?

c. What will you do in the future to communicate with your partner that his words don't match his actions? How will you hold him accountable?

d. How many times will you need to realize that your future or current partner's words and actions are misaligned, for you to give him walking papers? What did you choose that number?

MY ROAD TO HAPPINESS

_____

_____

_____

_____

_____

_____

_____

_____

_____

_____

_____

_____

_____

_____

_____

_____

_____

_____

_____

_____

_____

_____

_____

_____

_____

The Couple That Prays
Together, Stays Together

I know it sounds cliché, but I can attest to it. Bumblebee
and I created a tradition that included me leading the
blessing of the food, and her leading the blessing of our trav-
els. And after each prayer, we made certain to kiss. Of course,
it's some mushy and corny shit, but we felt it was important
to seal our conversation with the Lord in our own little way.

No matter what you believe or not believe in, it's impera-
tive that you and your partner have similar beliefs. Otherwise,
a house divided will likely lead to the demise of the relationship, no matter how much you like bumping uglies. I'm not
a big Bible thumper, but that damn Bumblebee…she knew
her stuff and could interpret scripture better than any tent
preacher.

Traditionally, a man is thought to be the spiritual leader
of the home. I was not. I deferred to Bumblebee because that
was her strong suit. I had no problem taking a backseat and
assuming the role of a student. This is another way to customize your relationship to fit you and not society. When your

185

partner has a skillset superior to yours, let them shine. That doesn't make you less of a leader in your own right. It makes you smart for understanding that you have deficiencies, and your partner is equipped to stand in the gap. Sometimes, you have to entrust your life's remote control to your partner. Together, you will build a healthy, powerful team. It is when we stopped praying together, that things began to go in the opposite direction for Bumblebee and me.

SELF-REFLECTION AND ACTION PLAN

a. How will you address any differences in religious beliefs with your current or future partner?

b. What religious traditions would you like to experience with your future or current partner?

c. In what ways have you entrusted your life's remote control to your partner?

d. What are you doing to be ready for the next chapter of your life?

MY ROAD TO HAPPINESS

Conclusion

I was fortunate to have had a wonderful partner in Bumblebee for six (6) years. We had our ups and downs, highs and lows; but when things were good, it was fucking amazing. This book was written from my heart, with a desire to help women gain a better understanding of opportunities to improve their relationships. I hope this read has inspired and motivated you to go the extra mile to know your man, foster a healthy dialogue with your current or future partner, and hold one another accountable when the mistakes are made. Mistakes are fine. It's how we handle those mistakes that will have you singing either, *Let's Stay Together* or *End of the Road*.

I recommend that you reflect on the answers you wrote in the Self-reflection and Action Plan sections and bring actions to those words. Relationships are work, hard work. But that work can be fun. Share your self-reflections with your current or future partner. What I'm saying here, is to be self-aware. Get in touch with who you genuinely are, not what your friends and the world want you to be. Accept yourself for who you are and how you want to be loved. Your current or future partner will then be able to love you, for better or for worse. It's time to courtesy flush your representative, just like when you're taking a mid-day shit at work.

As stated earlier, men are the dumbest species on Earth. We need women to help us understand how to love you. Based on what you learned in this book about the inner workings of men, I implore you to have those tough conversations with your partner; so you can improve your work toward a dynamic relationship like Bumblebee and I had - full of trust, understanding, teamwork, satisfaction, and love.

So you may ask, "If Bumblebee was all that, then why did you divorce?" My answer to that question is that I was just a good stand-in. Her heart was elsewhere, and the Lord eventually showed me that her representative was never flushed. It's all about the big 'A' word: *Accountability*. Absent ACCOUNTABILITY will more than likely lead to the big 'D' word: *Divorce*. That's a shameless plug for you to buy my next book. "Will your dawg ass just tell us the title of your next book," you ask? *The Big 'A' Word: Accountability*.